YOUR KNOWLEDGE HAS VALUE

Bibliographic information published by the German National Library:

The German National Library lists this publication in the National Bibliography; detailed bibliographic data are available on the Internet at http://dnb.dnb.de .

Imprint:

Copyright © 2019 GRIN Verlag
Print and binding: Books on Demand GmbH, Norderstedt Germany
ISBN: 9783346038234

This book at GRIN:

https://www.grin.com/document/502349

Hanna Treyer

Television as a Social Medium. New Usage Patterns and Future Scenarios

GRIN Verlag

GRIN - Your knowledge has value

Since its foundation in 1998, GRIN has specialized in publishing academic texts by students, college teachers and other academics as e-book and printed book. The website www.grin.com is an ideal platform for presenting term papers, final papers, scientific essays, dissertations and specialist books.

Visit us on the internet:

http://www.grin.com/

http://www.facebook.com/grincom

http://www.twitter.com/grin_com

Studiengang: Medien – und Kommunikationsmanagement

Medienmanagement, B.A.

Aktuelle Themen im Medienmanagement

Treyer Hanna

Table of Contents

1 Introduction

As soon as we get used to social networks and Internet-enabled smartphones, the cosiness of the living room is over. The leading medium TV is dethroned, Bill Gates even says: consecrated to death. In fact, television is upgrading and becoming a super-medium: highly networked, social and interactive, often in 3D, omnipresent, multifunctional and tailor-made (see Hirsch; Neef; Schroll, 2010). In the following work, current topics of the changed media landscape in the TV sector are described. In the further course of the work, the latest interactive film example from Netflix will be explained. And finally, there are forecasts for what recipients must expect in the future.

2 TV in upheaval: New usage patterns

More and more people are doing without a television set. They consume moving images via new channels, that have become available in the last ten years. The Internet makes TV reception on computers and mobile devices (smartphones, tablets, notebooks) possible and paves the way for two new developments: TV as a mobile experience is becoming reality; the parallel use of TV and the Internet is increasing. This simultaneous use of media has risen rapidly in recent years and shows the need for additional information for the TV experience. Usage patterns established on the Internet, are transferred to television. Compared to the many services, that dock to the moving image on the Internet, the linear television program as we know it today looks rather old-fashioned (see Winssen).

2.1 Main driver convergence: Social TV

The convergence of the Internet and TV is the main driver of change. It means two things: firstly, the transition from the broadcasting model to the infrastructure of the Internet and secondly, the integration of the moving image with the information and communication space of the World Wide Web. This change enables new services and thus a media experience, that has changed in many ways: the user himself makes the programme; the moving image is interwoven with the information offered by the web; personalization, interactivity and social TV are gaining in importance (see Buschow; Unterheide; Schneider, 2015).

With the analog video recorder, the viewer has already made himself independent of the broadcasting scheme; recording with the digital video recorder has opened further freedoms of interruption, of broadcasting and time-shifted reception. The world of the on-demand era is literally "programmeless" (see Hirsch; Neef; Schroll, 2010). In addition, the TV terminal is now multifunctional. The television set becomes the centre for house intelligence, a game centre and a conference system.

2.2 The glory of uniqueness

Television as a technical infrastructure is losing its independence in the age of convergence. But it is precisely this fact, that makes TV something special as an experience. In addition to active media use on the web, the user decides in favour of passive use and consciously allows himself to be sprinkled. The restrictions of the medium of television to one source, one time and one topic are becoming more attractive because they create a glory of uniqueness (see Hirsch; Neef; Schroll, 2010). More and more people feel the need, to experience television programmes in a community. In the live media event, the Internet has not at all served its purpose as the "electronic campfire of the global village community" (see Marshall McLuhan), which is most clearly demonstrated by the phenomenon of public viewing. Not only at World Cup football matches, but also on a smaller scale, for example at the Sunday crime scene in the pub. And parallel to the show, the viewer follows the reactions of others, to what they have seen on Twitter (see Hirsch; Neef; Schroll, 2010).

2.3 The end of stagnation

The thesis of Bill Gates' gloomy prognosis of the "death of television" is not right like that: It is true, however, that television will take on a whole new form. Compared with the rapid increase in intelligence of electronic everyday devices, such as PCs and smartphones, the capabilities of a television set have hardly changed in recent decades. In times of convergence, this stagnation is a thing of the past: the triad of a television set, remote control and program guide is virtually a phase-out model (see Hirsch; Neef; Schroll, 2010). The industry agrees: tomorrow's television will be completely different. The existing potential for change is enormous and creating completely new visual qualities. The old recipes are no longer enough to bind the viewer to the medium. The cards are being reshuffled and new players are beginning to make a lasting impression on the market. Innovation brakes will find it difficult to maintain their position (see Goldhammer, 2015).

3 Interactive Television

Anyone thinking of interactive television will probably have the image of their smartphone or tablet as a second screen in their head. Seven out of ten viewers use the devices parallel to the TV. They often talk to other users about the programmes on Twitter or search for information about the programme. For TV makers, this is the ideal way to involve viewers in their programme (see Tusch, 2017).

But interactive television isn't new, even before Twitter it was already there. Even now in the year 2000, the *"Tatort"* integrated the viewers into the plot. At the SWR crime scene *"Der Schwarze Ritter"*, viewers could go on a manhunt - provided they had a "F.U.N. Universal Decoder".

Parallel to the crime thriller, the decoder sent out questions which the viewer could answer using the remote control. Each user personally learned whether the answer was right or wrong.

3.1 With tweets on television

The whole thing was still quite cumbersome. But the concept was to evolve years later. Especially with Twitter, interactive television gained potential. In 2007, an MTV employee came up with the idea of having the music stars of the MTV Awards report on the event via Twitter. The principle was so well received, that the station expanded the concept over the next few years: soon the audience's tweets were integrated into the programme live via visualization. MTV had a reporter who reported on the audience's reactions to the show. A new kind of interaction was created.

Twitter is predestined for interaction with viewers precisely because of its speed. More and more stations are using hashtags to place the service prominently in their programmes, for example, the casting format *"The Voice of Germany"*. In this way, they can react to the audience and integrate them into their programme. It is also interesting to note, that this brings viewers back to linear television. After all, the exchange with others is only possible live (see Tusch, 2017).

In addition to Twitter, other methods are also suitable for involving viewers in the program: for example, apps. In 2012, the US television station ABC showed how it works. Using a special iPad app for the *"My Generation"* series, viewers could view background information, quiz questions or other information on the respective scene. In order to display the information correctly, the app recognized the viewer's current time by the sound of the series (see Patel, 2010).

The South Korean start-up *Sound.ly* has further developed this behaviour. A TV show can play out so-called sound Beacons, which the Smartphone or the tablet recognizes. However, humans can't hear these tones, which means the television set talks with the mobile phone. Thus, an App can play out information suitably to the sent program. If you watch a cooking show, for example, the smartphone offers the recipes. In a documentary film, an app could show background information on how the film was made. And if the viewer zaps to a home shopping channel, the smartphone opens the purchase options for the product (see Tusch, 2017).

3.2 How apps enhance the television experience

The app could create a bridge between the TV and the user that would allow much more interaction. The ProSieben knowledge magazine *Galileo* has already demonstrated this. The app did not recognize the TV by the sound, but by the camera of the smartphone. In a quiz, *Galileo* viewers were asked to point their smartphone camera at the television set and tap the answer on their mobile phone.

Then the app provides feedback as to whether the answer was correct. After the quiz, it shows who has become the "Galileo Quiz Champion" in the interactive quiz game (see galileo.tv, 2019).

The ARD programme *"Das Quizduell"* also called on viewers to puzzle. The viewers were able to answer the quiz questions of the show via an app. The audience's answers were shown immediately afterward in the studio and served as an orientation for the candidate.

"Das Quizduell" shows that the viewer's interaction with the programme is not only well received but also enriches the programmes themselves. After all, the audience is an elementary component of the show (see daserste.de, 2019).

However, this can also quickly backfire. Especially in the initial phase of the quiz duel, technical breakdowns caused trouble.

ARD recently demonstrated how to integrate viewers into feature films. Last year, with the film "Terror", the station showed the most sensational TV project to date with interactive elements. In the feature film, a court asked whether a pilot should be found guilty of 164 murders. The pilot shot a hijacked passenger plane from the sky before it possibly steered into the 70,000-strong Allianz Arena in Munich. Only the viewers voted on the outcome of the film, via app or telephone. 600,000 users registered for it. The project was a success (see daserste.de, 2019).

For the filmmakers, however, such a concept will open a whole new territory in the future. They must record numerous alternative plots, in which the viewer can move through the film along the options (see Tusch, 2017). This allows the viewer to decide whether a couple will come together or whether there will be a happy ending. Not a long time ago Netflix entered interactive television. Netflix has the advantage that the opinion of the individual counts. The viewer does not have to bow to the decision of the masses. Maybe this will make interactive television presentable in the first place (see DerTagesspiegel.de, 2019).

3.3 Netflix Black-Mirror movie Bandersnatch

In the movie the remote control becomes a joystick: Netflix makes the border between viewer and screen disappear. The movie "Black Mirror Bandersnatch" (since 28 December) is an interactive format for adults.

The highlight is, that you can control the plot of the movie from the couch via remote control or smartphone. The viewer lets the protagonist Stefan go either in one direction or the other - decisions of fate.

It starts with a decision: Sugar Puffs or rather Frosties? The viewer has barely ten seconds to decide by clicking, while a time display runs out at the bottom of the screen. What should 19-year-old Stefan Butler eat for breakfast?

The decision in Netflix's interactive film "Black Mirror: Bandersnatch" is up to the audience. Not all of them are as banal as the choice of the morning snack (see DerTagesspiegel.de, 2019).

Should Stefan take the job at a video game company or should he rather program in isolation from home? Talk to a psychotherapist about his feelings of guilt about his mother's death or suppress the topic? Jumping off a balcony during an LSD trip or persuading his work colleague Colin to commit suicide? This means that at certain forks the viewer chooses how to proceed. Then the selected storylines are played in. According to "Esquire", a total of 312 minutes of footage were shot for this. The actual length of the film at the end depends on the viewer's choice and can vary greatly. The "Independent" reports that the shortest version lasts 40 minutes, the longest two hours. In the end, there are five possible closing scenarios (see Meier, 2019).

For almost two years Netflix has been experimenting with programs between video games and movies. So far, this has only been content for children, for example the "Shrek" or "Minecraft Story Mode" series.

Decisions from the first episode had an impact on the subsequent episodes. With "Bandersnatch" and the story about a game developer who increasingly falls into madness and doubts the limits of his freedom of choice, the platform now for the first time also addresses an adult audience (see Tusch, 2017).

4 Future Television

"Deloitte" is a platform, in which thousands of experts work together in independent companies worldwide. Their aim is to advise selected clients in the areas of auditing, risk advisory, tax consulting and financial advisory.

In their study "*The future of the video and TV landscape in 2030*" Deloitte has identified several factors that will determine the future of the industry. There are four possible future scenarios for the TV and video industry for the year 2030. Each scenario focuses on a different player who has a decisive influence on the industry and will be described in the following.

4.1 Four future scenarios for 2030

The study "The future of the video and TV landscape in 2030" from Deloitte.

4.1.1 Universal Supermarket

In this scenario, the large digital platforms dominate the global market in all parts of the value chain. They are content producers, owners, and distributors. TV broadcasters only play a role in the production of national content and are not involved in distribution. Consumers have a large choice of global and national content, and differences between the providers only exist for a few exclusive productions and sports rights - such as in the large supermarkets, where the individual providers only differ in detail.

4.1.2 Content Endgame

The big winners in this scenario are the content owners. The role of digital platforms has undergone fundamental change. They are used almost exclusively for distribution, but consumers no longer pay for a provider, but directly for the content they want to see. Overall, the diversity of content has declined, while the quality of global offerings has reached new dimensions.

4.1.3 Revenge of the Broadcasters

TV broadcasters have mastered digitization and are able to offer on-demand content on a large scale and provide consumers with smart recommendations. In addition to broadcasters, digital platforms also continue to have their place in the market. While the former concentrate on high-quality local content, the latter deliver international productions and blockbusters. Consumers enjoy a rich content offering and can choose between linear and on-demand formats.

4.1.4 Lost in diversity

The TV and video market have developed into a differentiated ecosystem without a dominant player. Consumers are served by numerous different platforms with a correspondingly large variety of content. A lack of user loyalty drives the providers into a hard struggle for survival.

As different as the four future scenarios may be, they can nevertheless be used to derive overarching implications that will be relevant for all market participants. The changes of recent years already show, that no one can rest on established market positions. It would be wise if broadcasters and content producers were open to new alliances and cooperation's, even with direct competitors. Joint production, distribution models or even platforms are suitable measures, to counter the threat, posed by digital platform providers such as Netflix, Amazon, Apple and Google (see Deloitte.com, 2019).

5 Conclusion

Glass fibre, optic networks and 5G enable even more flexible and mobile use of media content in the future. Data analysis and artificial intelligence will improve recommendation functions. In addition, video-on-demand will become more widespread. Nevertheless, linear television will also be able to hold its own in the future, especially with live content, because most fans still want to be able to follow the finals of a football World Cup in real time. New and existing players will reposition themselves along the value chain in a partially consolidated global market.

Bibliography

- Buschhow, Christopher; Schneider, Beate. (2015): Social TV in Deutschland. Niedersächsiche Landesmedienanstalten
- Das Erste (2019). ARD Quiz App zum Downloaden. In https://www.daserste.de/unterhaltung/quiz-show/wer-weiss-denn-sowas/download-quiz-app100.html, viewed on 24.01.2019
- Der Tagesspiegel.de (2019). Netflix versucht sich am interaktiven Fernsehen. In https://www.tagesspiegel.de/gesellschaft/medien/black-mirror-bandersnatch-netflix-versucht-sich-am-interaktiven-fernsehen/23829502.html, viewed on 24.01.2019
- Galileo.tv (2019). Zum Ausprobieren: So schaust du Galilio in Augmented Reality. In https://www.galileo.tv/tech-trends/zum-ausprobieren-so-schaust-du-galileo-in-augmented-reality/, viewed on 24.01.2019
- Goldhammer, Klaus; Kerkau, Florian; Matejka, Moritz; Schlüter, Jan (2015). Social TV: Aktuelle Nutzung Prognosen, Konsequenzen. Schriftenreihe Medienforschung der Landesanstalt für Medien Nordrhein-Westfalen
- Hirsch, Sven; Neef, Andreas; Schroll, Willi. (2010): Eine Trendstudie von Z_punkt. TV 2020. Die Zukunft des Fernsehens. Köln: z_punkt GmbH
- Meier, Simone. (2019). Der interaktive «Black Mirror»-Film «Bandersnatch» ist Quatsch. Very bad job, Netflix! In https://www.watson.ch/leben/review/258154461-der-interaktive-black-mirror-film-bandersnatch-ist-quatsch-very-bad-job-netflix, viewed on 24.01.2019
- Patel, Kunur. (2010). ABC's Ipad watches My Generation along with you. In https://adage.com/article/media/digital-abc-ipad-app-generation-interactive-tv/145924/, viewed on 24.01.2019
- Van Winssen, Paul. (n.D.): The Rise of Social TV. In https://hub.uberflip.com/blog/the-rise-of-social-tv, viewed on 24.01.2019

YOUR KNOWLEDGE HAS VALUE